PsychSim 5

PsychSim 5

Interactive Graphic Simulation and Demonstration Activities for Psychology

Thomas E. Ludwig

Hope College

WORTH PUBLISHERS

PsychSim 5
Interactive Graphic Simulation and Demonstration Activities for Psychology
by Thomas E. Ludwig

Printed in the United States of America

ISBN: 0-7167-5741-9 (CD-ROM) (EAN: 9780716757412)
0-7167-5927-6 (Booklet) (EAN: 9780716759270)
0-7167-5957-8 (Booklet + CD-ROM) (EAN: 9780716759577)

Second Printing

Worth Publishers
41 Madison Avenue
New York, NY 10010
www.worthpublishers.com

Contents

Preface

PsychSim, an award-winning software from Thomas E. Ludwig, returns in a rich new iteration, bringing to life a wide range of psychology's core concepts and methods. This fifth edition, which contains more than twice the number of simulations as before, as well as updated animations and graphics, offers a unique way for students to better understand the major concepts of general psychology. These original interactive activities involve students in the practice of psychological research by having them play the role of an experimenter (conditioning a rat, probing the hypothalamus electrically, working in a sleep lab) or of a subject (responding to visual illusions or tests of memory, interpreting facial expressions). Other simulations provide dynamic tutorials or demonstrations of important principles and processes.

Features
PsychSim 5 contains the following features:

Simulated Experiments allow students to act as subject or experimenter in recreating experiments. The data are drawn from archival sources or collected on the spot from the student's responses. Results are explained after the experiment has been completed.

Interactive Demonstrations highlight key principles with animations, illustrations, and surveys—to reinforce important concepts in memorable ways. These activities emphasize a hands-on approach to learning, and provide coverage for all the major areas of psychology.

Digitized Video Demonstrations are author Thomas Ludwig's pedagogically effective combinations of instructional text, critical thinking questions, and video clips. The digitized video clips are a brief and effective means of bringing these key concepts to life.

Online Assessment Powered by Question Mark allows students to answer periodic critical thinking questions and receive instant feedback. Results are reported to instructors who can easily go into a protected Web site to view results by quiz, student, or question… or can get weekly results via E-mail.

Acknowledgments

Many people have assisted me in producing PsychSim 5. My colleagues and students at Hope College have been a great help in generating ideas for the activities. This edition of PsychSim has also benefited from the helpful comments and suggestions from many of the instructors who have used previous editions. I am particularly grateful to the reviewers of the previous edition: Steve Charlton, Kwantlen College; Pamela Costa, Tacoma Community College; Marian Gibney, Phoenix College; Colleen Pilgrim, Schoolcraft College; and Laura Reichel, Front Range Community College. In addition, I would like to thank Karen Clay Rhines of Seton Hall University for creating this set of worksheets. I also wish to extend my deep appreciation to the core team at Worth Publishers who have both supported me and offered creative direction in the production of this product. They are: Catherine Woods, publisher; Laura Pople, sponsoring editor; Danielle Pucci, media editor; Renee Altier and Kate Nurre, marketing managers; Kate Geraghty, Great Lakes regional sales manager; Meg Kuhta, photo researcher; and John Philp, video producer. I am also grateful to CADRE design for their development of this CD-ROM. Finally, I would like to thank my wife Debra for her support and her patience during this revision. Without her love and support this task would not have been possible.

Credits

Author:
Thomas E. Ludwig, Hope College

Additional Contributors:
Richard O. Straub, University of Michigan, Dearborn
Connie Varnhagen, University of Alberta
Charlotte vanOyen Witvliet, Hope College
Patricia Roehling, Hope College

Editors:
Catherine Woods
Laura Pople

Media Editor:
Danielle Pucci

Marketing Managers:
Renee Altier
Kate Nurre

Photo Research:
Meg Kuhta

Video Producer:
John Philp, Bad Dog Productions

Programming, animation, design, and development:
CADRE design

*Some elements of PsychSim 5 come from PsychOnline as developed by Sumanas, Inc.

System Requirements and Installation Instructions

Minimum System Requirements:
Windows
- Windows 95, 98, ME, NT, 2000, XP Operating System
- Pentium II Processor/266 MHz or faster
- 800x600 screen resolution or above
- 32 MB RAM
- 256 colors
- 4x CD-ROM

Macintosh
- OS 9 or OS X Operating System
- Power Macintosh G3 or G4 recommended/266 MHz or faster
- 800x600 screen resolution or above
- 32 MB RAM
- 256 colors
- 4x CD-ROM

Recommended Settings for *Windows* and *Macintosh*:
- 1024x768 screen resolution or above
- 64 MB RAM
- 8x CD-ROM

Installation Instructions: WINDOWS
1) Put the CD in the CD-ROM drive. Double click the "My Computer" icon on the Windows desktop and then double click the "PsychSim5" CD icon. Double-click on "PsychSim5.exe" to launch the program.

** Although you do not need a live Internet connection to run the program, you will need an Internet connection should you wish to submit your progress to your instructor.

Installation Instructions: MACINTOSH
1) Put the CD in the CD-ROM drive. Double click the "PsychSim5" CD icon that appears on your desktop then double click on "PsychSim5" to launch the program.

** Although you do not need a live Internet connection to run the program, you will need an Internet connection should you wish to submit your progress to your instructor.

***Please note that older Macintosh computers may be running a version of the Flash Player which requires CarbonLib version 1.3.1 or greater. For the program to start, CarbonLib will need to be installed. For more information, please see **http://www.macromedia.com/go/download_carbonlib**.

For technical support, call: 800-936-6899; or E-mail: techsupport@bfwpub.com

PsychSim 5

The PsychSim5 Activities

Psychology's Timeline

Purpose: To provide a more comprehensive synopsis of the origins of psychology, the early history of psychology as a discipline, and the major themes in twentieth century psychology

Summary: This activity will take you on a tour through the history of psychology. You will learn how psychology grew out of philosophy and medical physiology, and will become acquainted with some of the pioneers of psychology as a scientific discipline.

What's Wrong With This Study?

Purpose: To review some of the major pitfalls in designing a research study

Summary: In this activity you will review the basic methodology used in psychological research, practice applying research methodology to new situations, and consider specific pitfalls that could reduce the value of the research findings.

Descriptive Statistics

Purpose: To describe the common measures of central tendency and variability and demonstrate their use in summarizing a data set

Summary: This activity introduces you to the basic statistics that researchers use to summarize their sets of data. You will learn how to produce a distribution of scores and how to graph the distribution. After descriptions of the measures of central tendency (mode, median, and mean) and variability (range and standard deviation), you will be able to manipulate the scores in a distribution to see how each score affects the descriptive statistics for that distribution.

Correlation

Purpose: To demonstrate the use of scatterplots and to clarify the meaning of the correlation coefficient computed from them

Summary: This activity demonstrates the use of scatterplots to visualize positive and negative relationships. After reviewing the interpretation of positive and negative correlations, we'll test your skill at guessing the approximate value of correlation coefficients for various scatterplots. Then you'll be able to alter the scores in a data set to see the effects on the value of the correlation coefficient.

Neural Messages

Purpose: To describe and simulate the basic principles of axonal conduction and synaptic transmission in the nervous system

Summary: This activity explains the way neurons communicate with each other. You will review the basic types of neurons and the parts of a neuron, and then learn how neurons "fire" (generate impulses) and send messages to neighboring neurons.

Hemispheric Specialization

Purpose: To explain how research on split-brain patients has helped us understand the special abilities of the two halves of the brain

Summary: This activity describes what researchers have learned about the special abilities of the left and right sides of the brain. After a brief review of the way that information is carried from the main sensory channels to the brain, you will test the responses of a simulated "split-brain" patient to demonstrate that, for most right-handers, the main language center is located in the left hemisphere, and the right hemisphere is specialized for spatial tasks. Then you will carry out the same experiments with a simulated "normal" individual to explore the functioning of the hemispheres in an intact brain.

Brain and Behavior

Purpose: To review the major divisions of the brain (brainstem, cerebral cortex), the important structures within each region, and the chief functions of each brain structure or area

Summary: In this activity you will take a tour of the human brain, exploring the major brain regions to discover the functions of each region or area

Dating and Mating

Purpose: To explain evolutionary psychology's explanation of sex differences in mate selection

Summary: In this activity you will explore your own preferences for an "ideal mate," then consider the perspective of evolutionary psychology on this important issue.

Mind-Reading Monkeys

Purpose: To explain an important new research area that bridges the fields of evolutionary psychology, neuroscience, and social psychology

Summary: In this activity you will explore one of the brain mechanisms believed to foster the evolution of human language and culture. The focus of the activity is a simulated experiment in which you will play the role of a researcher who is recording the activity of "mirror neurons" in the premotor cortex of monkeys as they perform various tasks or watch others perform those tasks. The results will demonstrate that mirror neurons are involved in observational learning, and may have played a major role in the evolution of language and culture.

Cognitive Development

Purpose: To describe Piaget's theory on the growth of intelligence and simulate the performance of three children of different ages on some of Piaget's tasks

Summary: After presenting background information on Jean Piaget, this activity explains some of the basic concepts of his theory, including schemas, operations, and assimilation/accommodation. Next, Piaget's stages of cognitive development are described and illustrated with examples. In the last segment, you act as the experimenter, testing 4-, 7-, and 13-year-olds on Piaget's conservation and seriation tasks.

Conception to Birth

Purpose: To review the three phases of prenatal development, from the germinal phase (fertilization to about 2 weeks) through the embryonic phase (3 weeks to about 8 weeks) and the fetal phase (9 weeks to birth)

Summary: This activity will help you understand the sequence of prenatal development. You will take a tour through the three phases of development between conception and birth—with illustrations and animations of each stage of the process.

Who Am I?

Purpose: To review Erikson's perspective on identity formation and Marcia's categories of identity status during adolescence

Summary: This activity will help you understand Erik Erikson's perspective on identity formation, as well as James Marcia's four steps or stages in the identity process. The activity will also help you reflect on your own progress toward achieving a secure and stable identity.

Signs of Aging

Purpose: To explain the physical changes that occur in middle age and late adulthood

Summary: In this activity you will explore the main aspects of physical aging.

The Auditory System

Purpose: To explain how we hear and how the physical nature of the sound wave determines the quality of the sound experience

Summary: This activity covers the characteristics of sound that are important for hearing, and describes the structure of the ear and auditory pathway. You will be asked to locate the parts of the ear on a drawing. The activity simulates the transmission of a sound wave through the outer, middle, and inner ear and shows how the cochlea converts the mechanical energy to neural impulses. Next, it explains the concepts of frequency, amplitude, and waveform and shows how these aspects of the sound wave are related to the experience of pitch, loudness, and timbre.

Colorful World

Purpose: To review the principles of color sensation; includes a comparison of the trichromatic and opponent-process theories of color vision

Summary: In this activity you will explore the principles of color vision, and will demonstrate some aspects of color sensation with your own eyes.

Visual Illusions

Purpose: To demonstrate and explain four well-known visual illusions

Summary: This activity offers the opportunity to test your susceptibility to four famous visual illusions. In the Müller-Lyer, Ponzo, Horizontal-Vertical, and Poggendorf illusions you will be asked to adjust the length or position of one part of the stimulus to match the apparent length or position of another part. Your results will be displayed and interpreted.

Your Mind on Drugs

Purpose: To describe the basic types of psychoactive drugs and the neural mechanisms of drug action

Summary: In this activity you will explore the behavioral effects of some common drugs that influence the brain—producing changes in our arousal level, our mood, our perception of our environment, and our actions.

EEG and Sleep Stages

Purpose: To describe the five stages of the sleep cycle and the electroencephalograph (EEG)

Summary: This activity provides an explanation of physiological recording of electrical potentials from the scalp and their relationship to levels of consciousness and sleep, and is followed by a simulation of one night of recordings from a sleep laboratory, illustrating the normal sleep cycle, REM sleep, and the relationship between REM sleep and dream reports.

Maze Learning

Purpose: To demonstrate some principles of spatial learning and spatial memory in a way-finding task

Summary: This activity gives you a rat's-eye view of maze learning by allowing you to move and control a simulated rat's movements through a maze.

Classical Conditioning

Purpose: To simulate the acquisition and extinction of conditioned associations

Summary: This activity provides a review of Pavlov's famous experiment on the salivary response in dogs, as well as the basic processes of classical conditioning: acquisition, generalization, discrimination training, and extinction. You will play the role of an experimenter attempting to produce a conditioned eye blink in a human subject.

Operant Conditioning

Purpose: To demonstrate some principles of behavior control through the manipulation of reinforcement

Summary: This activity describes a form of learning called operant conditioning—learning from the consequences that follow our actions. The concept of reinforcement as illustrated with examples from everyday life, while the value of controlled reinforcement schedules is demonstrated in a simulated experiment showing rat bar-pressing behavior under four different schedules of reinforcement.

Monkey See, Monkey Do

Purpose: To introduce Albert Bandura's classic research on observational learning

Summary: In this activity you will learn about Albert Bandura's classic experiment on observational learning, will see some video clips of two children who participated in the experiment, and will be able to practice your skills in observing and labeling specific behaviors performed by these children.

Iconic Memory

Purpose: To demonstrate some aspects of sensory register

Summary: This activity simulates Sperling's classic experiments on the duration of visual sensory memory. You will see nine random letters flashed in a 3 x 3 matrix, and will attempt to recall the letters under three conditions: free-recall, cued-recall, and delayed cued-recall. Your results will be compared to Sperling's finding of rapid decay of the visual "icon."

Forgetting

Purpose: To demonstrate the effect of interference on memory

Summary: This activity will help you understand one of the reasons why we forget information—interference. After some introductory material, you will play the role of a subject in a simulated experiment on paired-associate learning.

Short-Term Memory

Purpose: To explain some basic aspects of short-term memory

Summary: In this activity you will learn about the common model of memory storage, and will be able to test your ability to hold information in short-term memory.

When Memory Fails

Purpose: To explain how memories are stored in the brain, and how damage to certain areas of the brain can impair memory

Summary: This activity explores severe memory loss—how it happens and what impact it has on behavior. In the process, you will learn about the different types of memories we store, as well as the areas of the brain that are involved in forming and retrieving memories.

Trusting Your Memory

Purpose: To explain research by Loftus, Schacter, Roediger, and others about memory errors based on gist memory, source confusion, and suggestibility

Summary: In this activity you'll be able to test the reliability of your memory, and then learn what researchers have discovered about the way that memories are stored and modified by new information.

My Head Is Spinning

Purpose: To demonstrate thinking with verbal concepts and mental images, using the concept of mental rotation

Summary: This activity provides some background information about thinking with verbal concepts versus thinking with mental images. The issue of mental rotation is introduced and explained with reference to the classic studies by Shepard and colleagues. You will participate in a simulated experiment involving mental rotation of the letter "R" in the picture plane. Your results will be graphed and compared with the pattern of results from Cooper and Shepard (1973).

Dueling Brains

Purpose: To examine research on hemispheric specialization and word recognition

Summary: This activity opens with a brief review of research on left-hemisphere specialization for language, and then presents a simulation of a classic word recognition experiment that typically demonstrates a right visual field advantage in identifying words.

Get Smart

Purpose: To explain the multidimensional nature of intelligence and demonstrate some tasks used to measure intelligence

Summary: In this activity you will explore the concept of intelligence and some of the methods of measuring intelligence. Along the way, you will try your hand at performing a few of the tasks and answering some questions typically found on intelligence tests.

Hunger and the Fat Rat

Purpose: To demonstrate the role of the hypothalamus in the control of eating behavior in rats

Summary: This activity provides a simulated experiment on weight regulation in rats. After a brief review of the methods of brain research involving electrical stimulation and destructive surgery, you will examine the effects of stimulating or destroying two different regions of a rat's hypothalamus. The results will be graphed in terms of the rat's daily food intake and body weight, illustrating the role of the hypothalamus in the regulation of eating and weight control.

Expressing Emotion

Purpose: To examine facial expressions and the underlying nonverbal messages they may convey

Summary: In this activity you will learn about the role of facial expressions in the nonverbal communication of emotion. Then we'll put you in control of a cartoon-type face and test your skill in manipulating its facial muscles to form particular emotional expressions. This will help you learn the facial cues associated with each primary emotion.

Catching Liars

Purpose: To explain the relationship between emotional states and physiological arousal, as revealed by nonverbal cues, facial expressions, and polygraph recordings

Summary: In this activity you will explore some of the methods used to detect deception.

All Stressed Out

Purpose: To provide an overview of the bio-psycho-social nature of stress, including its everyday sources, the psychological and physiological impact of stressors, and how cognitive appraisal influences the coping process

Summary: This activity will describe for you the sources of everyday stress. Next, you'll read a description of the impact of stress on the mind and body, focused on the fight-or-flight response (and its possible variant, *tend and befriend*). Then, you will learn about the most influential model describing stress as a process—the *transactional model*. Finally, you will complete an interactive exercise exploring how differences in cognitive appraisal and coping style alter the stress experience.

Helplessly Hoping

Purpose: To explain the research basis for the concept of learned helplessness

Summary: In this activity you will explore the importance of a sense of personal control over the events in your life. You'll participate in a simulated experiment on learned helplessness in dogs, and then consider how the results might apply to the behavior of people trapped in unpleasant situations.

Mystery Client

Purpose: To review and test understanding of the classification of behavioral disorders

Summary: This activity will be most useful to you after you have read the text material on psychological disorders. In this activity you'll take the role of a consultant called in to provide a second opinion on several clients with disorders, based only on the information contained in the clients' files. You will select the information to be examined for each client, then form a diagnosis according to what you know about the symptoms of the various disorders.

Losing Touch With Reality

Purpose: To explain the symptoms of schizophrenia and the brain changes that accompany schizophrenia

Summary: This activity explores schizophrenia, one of the most severe and bizarre psychological disorders. You will learn about the types of schizophrenia and the main symptoms, view video clips of individuals with schizophrenia, and be asked to identify the symptoms displayed by each individual.

Computer Therapist

Purpose: To demonstrate (in a limited way) some principles of active listening and artificial intelligence by having the computer simulate a Rogerian person-centered therapist

Summary: After learning about the famous ELIZA artificial intelligence program, you will engage in a conversation with a "computer therapist." The "therapist" will respond in a more-or-less realistic fashion, by identifying key words or phrases in your conversation, and then generating a nonjudgmental reply that reflects your feelings, to simulate some principles of active listening from Carl Roger's client-centered therapy.

Mystery Therapist

Purpose: To help students understand the basic goals and techniques of the main forms of psychotherapy

Summary: The activity reviews the major perspectives on psychological disorders and therapy and presents an interactive exercise in which students read brief fragments of case studies and are asked to identify the type of therapy exemplified by each case.

Social Decision-Making

Purpose: To demonstrate the decision-making strategies of persons in zero-sum and non-zero-sum environments

Summary: This activity contains a simulation of two classic "social trap" games used in research on competition and cooperation. You will first play the "Prisoner's Dilemma" game against the computer, and will quickly discover the difference between zero-sum and non-zero-sum environments. Next, you will play the "Trucking Game" against the computer to explore ways to maximize trust and cooperation in situations where people compete for limited resources.

Not My Type

Purpose: To examine the research on attribution and person perception

Summary: In this activity, after reviewing some of the research on the impact of "first impressions," you will explore the process of forming attitudes about other people.

Everybody's Doing It!

Purpose: To help students understand the pressure to conform to the behavior of others

Summary: In this activity you will explore the issue of social influence—how the behavior of other people affects your behavior. We'll take you through simulations of some of the classic experiments on conformity and apply the results to everyday situations.

PsychSim 5: PSYCHOLOGY'S TIMELINE

Name: _____   Section: _____

Date: _____

This activity will take you on a tour through the history of psychology. You will learn how psychology grew out of philosophy and medical physiology, and will become acquainted with some of the pioneers of psychology as a scientific discipline.

Famous Psychologists
- Can you think of any famous psychologists from psychology's history?

The Early History: Philosophers and Scientists
- Match each of the philosophers and scientists with their descriptions AND write in the approximate year of their contribution.

o _____ Aristotle (_____)	320 B.C.	A. British philosopher, empiricist
o _____ Darwin (_____)	360 B.C.	B. Greek philosopher, nativist
o _____ Descartes (_____)	1600	C. British biologist
o _____ Helmholz (_____)	1700	D. German physiologist
o _____ Locke (_____)	1830	E. French philosopher, nativist, and dualist
o _____ Plato (_____)	1860	F. Greek philosopher, empiricist

Pioneers of Psychology
- Match each of the pioneers of psychology with their descriptions AND write in the approximate year of their main contribution.

o _____ Calkins (_____)	1879	A. Studied memory
o _____ Ebbinghaus (_____)	1882	B. First psychotherapy
o _____ Freud (_____)	1885	C. First lab in USA
o _____ Hall (_____)	1888	D. Used introspection
o _____ James (_____)	1890	E. First comprehensive textbook
o _____ Titchener (_____)	1895	F. First psychology laboratory
o _____ Wundt (_____)	1900	G. First woman president of APA

Twentieth Century Psychology
- Match each of the key contributors with their descriptions AND write in the approximate year of their main contribution.

o	_____ Chomsky (_____)	1905	A. Studied learning in cats
o	_____ Maslow (_____)	1910	B. First woman PhD
o	_____ Pavlov (_____)	1915	C. Discovered conditioning
o	_____ Piaget (_____)	1920	D. Founded behaviorism
o	_____ Rogers (_____)	1940	E. Studied reinforcement
o	_____ Skinner (_____)	1950	F. Studied children's intelligence
o	_____ Thorndike (_____)	1955	G. Studied language
o	_____ Washburn (_____)	1960	H. Humanist approach
o	_____ Watson (_____)	1970	I. Humanistic therapy

PsychSim 5: WHAT'S WRONG WITH THIS STUDY?

Name: _____   **Section:** _____

Date: _____

In this activity you will review the basic methodology used in psychological research, practice applying research methodology to new situations, and consider specific pitfalls that could reduce the value of the research findings.

Thinking About Psychological Research
- What are the three types of research methods and what are their goals?

    1. Type:

        Goals:

    2. Type:

        Goals:

    3. Type:

        Goals:

Experimental Control
- What is the benefit of conducting an experiment, rather than using a different type of study?

Study 1: Vocabulary Growth
- What is the broad goal of the study?

- What is wrong with the study?

- In your own words, describe the single most important flaw in this study's design or interpretation.

- In your own words, describe how the study could be improved to eliminate the weaknesses (or at least the major flaw).

Study 2: Learning to Share
- What is the broad goal of the study?

- What is wrong with the study?

- In your own words, describe the single most important flaw in this study's design or interpretation.

- In your own words, describe how the study could be improved to eliminate the weaknesses (or at least the major flaw).

Study 3: Sleep and Academic Performance
- What is the broad goal of the study?

- What is wrong with the study?

- In your own words, describe the single most important flaw in this study's design or interpretation.

- In your own words, describe how the study could be improved to eliminate the weaknesses (or at least the major flaw).

Study 4: Language Instruction
- What is the broad goal of the study?

- What is wrong with the study?

- In your own words, describe the single most important flaw in this study's design or interpretation.

- In your own words, describe how the study could be improved to eliminate the weaknesses (or at least the major flaw).

PsychSim 5: DESCRIPTIVE STATISTICS

Name: _____   **Section:** _____

Date: _____

This activity introduces you to the basic statistics that researchers use to summarize their sets of data.

The numbers below represent the scores of a group of students on a math test. Use them to perform the required calculations.

10, 13, 10, 12, 11, 7, 12, 11, 6, 11, 12, 11, 8, 10, 9

Distribution of Scores
- Sort the scores; that is, arrange them in order from lowest to highest.

- Create a frequency histogram.

Measures of Central Tendency
- What is a mode?

- What is the mode of your distribution? _____

- What is a median?

- What is the median of your distribution? _____

Measures of Central Tendency *(continued)*
- What is a mean?

- How is a mean calculated?

- What is the mean of your distribution? _____ Show your calculations.

Skewed Distributions
- Which measure of central tendency would be the best "average" to describe a skewed distribution? Why?

Measures of Variability
- How is a range calculated?

- What is the range of your distribution? _____

- What is standard deviation?

- How is standard deviation calculated?

PsychSim 5: CORRELATION

Name: _____   Section: _____

Date: _____

This activity demonstrates the use of scatterplots to visualize positive and negative relationships.

Positive Correlation
- What does it mean to say that two variables are positively correlated?

Negative Correlation
- What does it mean to say that two variables are negatively correlated?

Uncorrelated Variables
- What does it mean to say that two variables are uncorrelated?

Correlation Coefficient
- What is a correlation coefficient?

Why Use It?
- What value or benefit would a researcher gain by calculating a correlation coefficient rather than simply describing the relationship as a positive correlation or a negative correlation?

Estimating the Relationship
- Look at the scatterplots and try to estimate the direction (positive or negative) and the strength of the relationship. Write in your guess below.

    o Scatterplot 1 _____   o Scatterplot 4 _____

    o Scatterplot 2 _____   o Scatterplot 5 _____

    o Scatterplot 3 _____   o Scatterplot 6 _____

Causality and Predictability
- The presence of a correlation between two variables doesn't prove that certain values on one variable _____ high or low values on the other. It merely demonstrates that the two variables are _____ in some way.
- The relationship between two correlated variables has _____.
  This means that if a strong correlation exists between variables, then knowing a person's score on one variable allows us to predict a person's score on the other variable.

PsychSim 5: NEURAL MESSAGES

Name: _____   **Section:** _____

Date: _____

This activity explains the way that neurons communicate with each other.

Neuron Parts

Match the part of the neuron identified with its description:

- o   ___ Axon

    A. Contains the nucleus, which controls the
       function of the entire cell

- o   ___ Axon terminals

    B. Carry signals to other nerve cells

- o   ___ Cell body (soma)

    C. Receive signals from other nerve cells

- o   ___ Dendrites

    D. Contain small sacs called synaptic vesicles
       that play an important role in transmitting signals from
       one cell to the next

A Tip

- Dendrites _____

- Axons _____

A Closer Look

- What does it mean to say that an axon's membrane is "selectively permeable?"

- Given what you know about synaptic transmission, how do you think a message jumps across the synaptic gap and is passed to the next neuron?

PsychSim 5: HEMISPHERIC SPECIALIZATION

Name: _____   **Section:** _____

Date: _____

This activity describes what researchers have learned about the special abilities of the left and right sides of the brain. You will learn how information is transmitted to these two hemispheres and about the unique function of each.

Hemispheric Connections

- What is the name of the band of fibers connecting the left and right hemispheres of the brain? What is its function?

- Each hemisphere is primarily connected to the opposite side of the body. This means that a touch on the *left* hand would be registered in which hemisphere?

- When sound waves enter the *right* ear, which hemisphere receives the primary information?

- This crossover pattern is also true in part for the visual pathway. When light enters the *left* eye, which hemisphere receives the information?

- How is the visual pathway from the eye *different* from that of the ear or hand?

Split-Brain Research

- Briefly explain split-brain research.

- If a participant is blindfolded and a fork is placed in his or her *right* hand, how would you guess that the person would respond?

- If a participant is blindfolded and a fork is placed in his or her *left* hand, how would you guess that the person would respond?

Split-Brain Research (continued)

- A split-brain patient can name an unseen object placed in the right hand, but cannot name objects placed in the left hand. What does this suggest about the language abilities of the two hemispheres?

- In an additional experiment, words are flashed briefly to the left or right visual field of the participant. Try to predict the results. For example, when the word appears in the *left* visual field, will the person be able to read the word?

- In a different task, a split-brain patient has to look at a completed block pattern and assemble the blocks near his or her *right* hand to match the pattern, using only the *right* hand. Can the patient do it? Explain your thinking.

- Why is it that normal humans (with an intact corpus callosum) can name objects placed in either hand and easily read words flashed to either visual field?

PsychSim 5: BRAIN AND BEHAVIOR

Name: _____   Section: _____

Date: _____

In this activity you will take a tour of the human brain and explore the major brain regions to discover the functions of each region or area.

Functional Specialization

- In terms of brain function, what is functional specialization?

- Why is the principle of complex communication important to understand?

Test Yourself on Lower Brain Structures

- Match each brain part with its function:

o ___ Pituitary gland	A. Located above the midbrain at the top of the brainstem; routes incoming messages from all the senses (except smell) to the appropriate brain areas for processing
o ___ Medulla	B. Part of the limbic system; regulates hunger, thirst, and body temperature and contains the so-called pleasure centers of the brain
o ___ Pons	C. The master gland of the endocrine system
o ___ Reticular formation	D. Located in the brainstem; controls breathing and heartbeat
o ___ Cerebellum	E. A nerve network that runs up the center of the brainstem; plays an important role in controlling alertness and attention
o ___ Midbrain	F. Located at the back of the brainstem; assists in balance and the coordination of voluntary movement
o ___ Thalamus	G. Part of the limbic system; is involved in learning and in forming new memories
o ___ Hippocampus	H. Part of the limbic system; is involved in regulation of the emotions of fear and rage
o ___ Amygdala	I. Located near the top of the brainstem; integrates specific types of information from the eyes and the ears, and sends this on to other parts of the brain
o ___ Hypothalamus	J. Located in the brainstem; controls breathing and heartbeat; connects the medulla to the two sides of the cerebellum to help coordinate and integrate movement on each side of the body; involved in sleep and dreaming

The Cerebral Cortex
- Each hemisphere of the cerebral cortex is divided into four regions called "lobes." Name them. Match each lobe to its associated cortex:

  o ___ _____   A. Somatosensory cortex

  o ___ _____   B. Motor cortex

  o ___ _____   C. Visual cortex

  o ___ _____   D. Auditory cortex

The Cerebral Cortex
- Name the three distinct areas of language cortex in the left hemisphere. Match them to their related dysfunction.

  o ___ _____   A. Ability to read aloud

  o ___ _____   B. Speaking

  o ___ _____   C. Language comprehension

Right Hemisphere Abilities
- If the left hemisphere generally controls language, what special abilities does the right hemisphere have?

PsychSim 5: DATING AND MATING

Name: _____   Section: _____

Date: _____

In this activity you will explore your own preferences for an "ideal mate," and then consider the perspective of evolutionary psychology on this important issue.

Why Do People Fall in Love?
- What three factors have social psychologists concluded most influence romantic attraction?

    1.

    2.

    3.

Results From the Ideal Romantic Partner Survey
- Did any of the research results surprise you? If not, isn't that fact surprising in itself?

Gender Differences in Mate Selection
- Across cultures, men consistently place more value than women do on a potential mate's _____, _____, and _____.

- Women consistently place more value than men do on attracting _____, _____, _____, _____ mates; women also want mates who will make a _____ in their offspring.

Evolutionary Explanations of Mate Selection
- Does the evolutionary perspective on mate selection make sense to you, or do you see weaknesses in these explanations?

Making Up and Breaking Up: Jealousy
- What is the evolutionary explanation for gender differences in jealousy?

Evaluating Evolutionary Explanations
- What are some of the weaknesses of the evolutionary perspective on mate selection?

PsychSim 5: MIND-READING MONKEYS

Name: _____   **Section:** _____

Date: _____

This activity explores one of the brain mechanisms believed to foster the evolution of human language and culture. The focus of the activity is a simulated experiment in which you will play the role of a researcher who is recording the activity of "mirror neurons" in the premotor cortex of monkeys as they perform various tasks or watch others perform those tasks.

Brain Regions

- Briefly describe the premotor cortex of the brain, including its location and function.

Neural Experiments

- In the first simulated experiment with Rizzo, a macaque monkey, a wooden block is placed in front of him and the results of his neural activity are graphed. What does the graph tell you about the activity of this neuron while Rizzo performed the action of grasping a wooden block? Does it appear that this neuron is "tuned" to respond to this particular action?

- In the second simulated experiment with Rizzo, a small raisin is placed in front of him and the results of his neural activity are graphed. What does the graph tell you about the activity of this neuron while Rizzo performed the action of grasping a raisin? Does it appear that this neuron is "tuned" to respond to this particular action?

- In the final simulated experiment with Rizzo, the experimenter grasps a small raisin while Rizzo watches. The results of his neural activity are graphed. What does the graph tell you about the activity of this neuron while Rizzo watched the experimenter perform the action of grasping a raisin? What purpose could this neuron serve?

Mirror Neurons

- What purpose or purposes could mirror neurons serve in human behavior?

- What is the theorized role of mirror neurons in relation to empathy?

PsychSim 5: COGNITIVE DEVELOPMENT

Name: _____   **Section:** _____

Date: _____

This activity describes Piaget's theory of the growth of intelligence and simulates the performance of three children of different ages on some of Piaget's tasks.

Schemas
- What are schemas?

- Explain the difference between assimilation and accommodation.

- Suppose that a 15-month-old toddler has learned to call the four-legged house pet a "doggie." What do you think would happen if the child sees a horse for the first time? Is the child likely to call the horse a "horsie" or a "doggie" or a "doggie-horse" or some other term? Write your best guess in the space below, and add a sentence explaining why you think the child would use that term to refer to the horse.

Stages of Development
- What are some characteristics of a child in the sensorimotor stage of development? What is object permanence?

- What are some cognitive limitations of preschoolers? What is egocentrism?

- A child in the concrete operations stage can reason differently than can a child in the sensorimotor stage. For example, if shown two identical balls of clay, one of which has been rolled into a rope, an older child (in the concrete operational period) might decide that the ball and the rope both have the same amount of clay. What kinds of reasoning do you think the older child might use to draw that conclusion?

Measures of Mental Operations

- What are some differences in mental operations among the three children in the conservation of number/checkers task?

- What are some differences in mental operations among the three children in the conservation of liquid/water glass task?

- What are some differences in mental operations among the three children in the seriation/sticks task?

- What are some differences in mental operations among the three children in the seriation without visible objects/word problem task?

PsychSim 5: CONCEPTION TO BIRTH

Name: _____   **Section:** _____

Date: _____

This activity will help you understand the sequence of prenatal development.

Fertilization
- Of the 200 to 400 million sperm cells released in a typical ejaculation, approximately how many do you think will reach the ovum?

    _____ 100   _____ 3000   _____ 100,000   _____ 1,000,000

Germinal Phase
- Briefly describe the main features of this phase of development.

Embryonic Phase
- Briefly describe the main features of this phase of development.

Fetal Phase
- Briefly describe the main features of this phase of development.

Summary
- Now that you have viewed the entire sequence of prenatal development, what do you think are the most important themes of development during these 38 weeks?

PsychSim 5: WHO AM I?

Name: _____   **Section:** _____

Date: _____

This activity will help you understand Erik Erikson's perspective on identity formation, as well as James Marcia's four steps or stages in the identity process.

Your Results
- What was your exploration score? _____

- What was your commitment score? _____

Paths to Identity Achievement
- How did Erikson define identity achievement? What combination of exploration and commitment scores are seen?

- What is diffusion? What combination of exploration and commitment scores are seen?

- What is foreclosure? What combination of exploration and commitment scores are seen?

- What is moratorium? What combination of exploration and commitment scores are seen?

Marcia's Identity Status Model
- After considering your identity status classification based on the initial questionnaire, do you believe that your classification was accurate?

- Which of Marcia's four statuses best fits you right now?

- Why you would not classify yourself as being in the other three statuses?

PsychSim 5: SIGNS OF AGING

Name: _____   **Section:** _____

Date: _____

In this activity you will explore the main aspects of physical aging.

Aging Begins in Early Adulthood
- What distinctions do researchers find between primary and secondary aging?

Aging and Appearance
- List four changes in appearance experienced with aging:

    1.

    2.

    3.

    4.

Sensory Changes
- List the two senses most significantly affected by aging:

    1.

    2.

Physical Functioning
- Name two of the changes in physical functioning experienced during aging:

    1.

    2.

Conclusion: Making the Most of Each Stage
- How will you feel about the changes that aging brings? Which of the changes will bother you the most?

PsychSim 5: THE AUDITORY SYSTEM

Name: _____   **Section:** _____

Date: _____

This activity explores how we hear and how the physical nature of the sound wave determines the quality of the sound experience.

The Auditory System
- What are the four tasks of the auditory system?

    1.

    2.

    3.

    4.

Structure of the Ear
- What are the three main regions of the ear and their associated parts?

    1.

    2.

    3.

The Sound Wave
- How are sound waves like ocean waves?

- What are the three aspects of sound waves?

    1.

    2.

    3.

Frequency: The Rate of Vibration

- Which type of tuning fork would vibrate faster—a small, short one or a large, long one? Why?

- How is frequency measured and calculated?

Frequency, Amplitude, and Waveform

- The frequency of a sound wave determines the _____ of the sound we perceive.

- The amplitude of a sound wave determines the _____ of the sound we perceive.

- The waveform of a sound wave determines the _____ of the sound we perceive.

Hearing Sounds

- What happens inside the cochlea?

PsychSim 5: COLORFUL WORLD

Name: _____   **Section:** _____

Date: _____

In this activity you will explore the principles of color vision, and will demonstrate some aspects of color sensation with your own eyes.

The Sensation of Color
- Name and briefly describe the three sensations of color.

    1.

    2.

    3.

Mixing Colored Lights: Additive Mixing
- What color appears when you combine all three lights?

Mixing Colored Pigments: Subtractive Mixing
- What color appears when you combine all three pigments?

Altering Color Sensation
- If you stare at a red patch and then look at a red apple, will your experience of the "redness" of the apple be stronger or weaker? Why?

Conclusion
- Explain how the two main theories of color perception, initially appearing to contradict each other, are, in fact, complementary perspectives.

PsychSim 5: VISUAL ILLUSIONS

Name: _____   **Section:** _____

Date: _____

This activity offers the opportunity to test your susceptibility to four famous illusions by having you adjust the length or position of one part of the stimulus to match the apparent length or position of another part.

The Müller-Lyer Illusion

- What were your results on the Müller-Lyer Illusion test? _____

- How is this illusion related to depth perception?

- What were your results on the second Müller-Lyer Illusion test? _____

- Was your pattern of performance similar to the first set of trials, or did the explanation of the illusion affect your performance? Describe your performance on the two sets of trials, indicating whether you did anything on the second set of trials to compensate for the illusion.

The Ponzo Illusion

- What were your results on the Ponzo Illusion test? _____

- How is this illusion related to size constancy and depth perception?

- Considering the explanation for this illusion, would you expect this illusion to be affected by culture? Explain your answer.

- What were your results on the second Ponzo Illusion test? _____

- Did knowing the cause of this illusion help you overcome your susceptibility to it on your second trial? Explain your thinking.

The Horizontal-Vertical Illusion
- What were your results on the Horizontal-Vertical Illusion test? _____

- What are the two factors related to this illusion?

- What were your results on the second Horizontal-Vertical Illusion test? _____

- Did knowing the cause of this illusion help you overcome your susceptibility to it on your second trial? Explain your thinking.

The Poggendorf Illusion
- What were your results on the Poggendorf Illusion test? _____

- How is this illusion related to depth perception?

- What were your results on the second Poggendorf Illusion test? _____

- Did knowing the cause of this illusion help you overcome your susceptibility to it on your second trial? Explain your thinking.

PsychSim 5: YOUR MIND ON DRUGS

Name: _____   Section: _____

Date: _____

In this activity you will explore the behavioral effects of some common drugs that influence the brain—producing changes in our arousal level, our mood, our perception of our environment, and our actions.

How Do Psychoactive Drugs Work?

- What are the main ways drugs get into our bloodstream? What are the three phases of drug effects?

Drugs and Neurotransmitters

- How are psychoactive drugs categorized? Name one example of a drug in each of the three main categories.

- Explain the difference between drug agonists and drug antagonists.

Drug Tolerance

- What is drug tolerance? What are the two reasons for the development of tolerance?

Addiction Experiment

- After experimenting with the injection of various solutions into specific areas of a rat's brain and observing the subsequent bar-pressing behavior, what conclusions did you draw from the rat's behavior? What type of injection seemed to be more pleasurable for the rat? Did the location of the injection make a difference?

PsychSim 5: EEG AND SLEEP STAGES

Name: _____   **Section:** _____

Date: _____

This activity provides an explanation of the measurement of brain activity, as well as the presence of different sleep patterns and their respective functions.

EEG
- How is the brain's electrical activity recorded?

Stages of Sleep
- Complete the following table:

	Characteristic	EEG Pattern
Stage 1		
Stage 2		
Stage 3		
Stage 4		
REM Sleep		

Sleep Thoughts Versus True Dreams
- If people have vivid, realistic dreams during REM sleep, why don't they act out those dreams, perhaps injuring themselves or others?

Purpose of Sleep
- What are the two main purposes of sleep?

PsychSim 5: MAZE LEARNING

Name: _____   **Section:** _____

Date: _____

This activity gives you a rat's-eye view of maze learning by allowing you to move and control a simulated rat's movements through a maze.

Which Model Fits Your Behavior?
- Take a moment to think about what approach you would use to find your way across campus, perhaps from your psychology class to some other building. Put your way-finding strategy into words.

- Does your model fit better with the chained associations model or the cognitive map model?

    ___ Chained associations

    ___ Cognitive map

Results for Maze A
- Did you feel that you were memorizing a sequence of turns, or that you were forming a cognitive map of the maze?

    ___ Sequence of turns

    ___ Cognitive map

Results for Maze B
- Compare the number of moves and the path you took in the first run with your performance in the second run. Did you get better with practice? Did you use the same strategy that you used on the Maze A, or did you try a different approach?

How Does Maze Learning Occur?
- What brain structure controls all types of spatial learning?

PsychSim 5: CLASSICAL CONDITIONING

Name: _____   **Section:** _____

Date: _____

This activity provides a review of Pavlov's famous experiment on the salivary response in dogs, as well as the basic processes of classical conditioning: acquisition, generalization, discrimination training, and extinction.

Salivary Response
- In Pavlov's famous experiment, what did he call the...

    o unconditioned stimulus (UCS)? _____

    o unconditioned response (UCR)? _____

    o conditioned stimulus (CS)? _____

    o conditioned response (CR)? _____

A New Salivary Response
- Pavlov demonstrated that the dog had formed a conditioned association between two events. What were those events? What did the dog actually learn?

Acquisition
- In the example of a child who fears doctors, what label would you give to the painful injection?

    _____ UCS   _____ UCR   _____ CS   _____ CR

- In the example of a child who fears doctors, what label would you give to the presence of the doctor?

    _____ UCS   _____ UCR   _____ CS   _____ CR

Demonstrating Acquisition
- How could we demonstrate that acquisition had occurred—that is, demonstrate that the child had learned the link between the doctor and the injection?

Extinction

- What is extinction?

- What is spontaneous recovery?

Generalization

- What is generalization?

Discrimination

- What is discrimination?

Conditioning an Eye Blink

- What is the CR in this example? _____

- What is the CS in this example? _____

- What is the UCS in this example? _____

- What is the UCR in this example? _____

Experiment Simulation

- Why are we interested only in the blinks that occur before the puff of air?

Discrimination Trials

- How would you interpret these graphs? Did your subject show evidence of stimulus generalization, or stimulus discrimination, or both?

Extinction Trials

- How would you interpret these results? Has the conditioned response been extinguished in your subject? What would happen if we continued immediately with more trials? What would happen if we brought her back to the laboratory tomorrow for more trials?

PsychSim 5: OPERANT CONDITIONING

Name: _____   **Section:** _____

Date: _____

This activity describes a form of learning called operant conditioning—learning from the consequences that follow our actions.

Classical Versus Operant Conditioning

- What is the distinction between classical and operant conditioning?

Reinforcement and Punishment

- What effect does reinforcement have on behavior?

- Give an example of positive reinforcement.

- Give an example of negative reinforcement.

- What effect does punishment have on behavior?

- Give an example of punishment.

Continuous Versus Partial Reinforcement

- If a subject comes to expect a reward after every response, what will happen if the reinforcement stops?

Schedules of Reinforcement

- Define the following schedules of reinforcement and give an everyday example of each:

    o   Fixed ratio

    o   Fixed interval

    o   Variable ratio

    o   Variable interval

Simulated Experiment: Schedules of Reinforcement

- Which schedule of reinforcement is MOST resistant to extinction? Why do you think this is so?

PsychSim 5: MONKEY SEE, MONKEY DO

Name: _____   **Section:** _____

Date: _____

In this activity you will learn about Albert Bandura's classic experiment on observational learning.

Results from Bandura's Experiment
- What did Bandura's results show about the relationship between direct reward and punishment and learning? What is this process called?

A Closer Look at Bandura's Experiment
- List the specific behaviors seen in the movie clip:

Observing the Children Who Observed the Model
- List the specific behaviors of the boy seen in the movie clip:

Observing the Children Who Observed the Model
- List the specific behaviors of the girl seen in the movie clip:

Inventing Novel Behaviors
- What two things did Bandura conclude that children learn from observing an aggressive model?

    1.

    2.

PsychSim 5: ICONIC MEMORY

Name: _____   **Section:** _____

Date: _____

This activity simulates Sperling's classic experiments on the duration of visual sensory memory.

Free Recall Test
- What was your score on the free recall test? _____

Iconic Memory
- What is Sperling's theory of iconic memory? What is an "icon?"

- What is Sperling's partial report task? How does it test his theory of iconic memory?

Partial Report Test
- What was your score on the partial report test? _____

- Are your results consistent or inconsistent with typical results? What do typical results suggest?

Delayed Partial Report Test
- What was your score on the delayed partial report test? _____

- What does the typical drop in performance tells us about the duration of iconic memory?

PsychSim 5: FORGETTING

Name: _____   **Section:** _____

Date: _____

This activity will help you understand one of the reasons why we forget information – interference.

Encoding Failure
- What does an encoding failure mean in terms of memory?

Encoding Example
- Did you remember the duplicate letter? _____

- Why do most people have difficulty with this task?

Other Failures
- What other explanations are there for our failure to recall information at a later time?

Comparing the Results
- How did your results differ on Trial 1 versus Trial 2?

Other Types of Interference
- Name and briefly describe two types of interference that affect memory during processing and storage.

    1.

    2.

Paired-Associates Study Trials
- What was your score on Test 1? _____

- What was your score on Test 2? _____

- What was your score on Test 3? _____

What did your results on the three trials indicate?

PsychSim 5: SHORT-TERM MEMORY

Name: _____   **Section:** _____

Date: _____

In this activity you will learn about the common model of memory storage.

Capacity of Short-Term Memory
- What is the "magical number" in terms of short-term memory (STM)? What does this mean?

Chunking Expands STM Capacity
- What is "chunking?"

- Give an everyday example of chunking.

STM Format or Code
- Can the auditory code used in STM help explain why people have a slightly better memory for random lists of seven digits (0–9) than for random lists of seven letters (A–Z)?

PsychSim 5: WHEN MEMORY FAILS

Name: _____   Section: _____

Date: _____

This activity explores severe memory loss—how it happens and what impact it has on behavior.

Forms of Long-Term Memory
- Researchers believe that there are distinct forms of long-term memory, each designed to handle specific types of information or experiences. Match the name of the form to its description below.

    o ___ Explicit Memory

    o ___ Implicit Memory

    o ___ Semantic Memory

    o ___ Episodic Memory

    o ___ Procedural Memory

    o ___ Conditioned Response

A. Behaviors or emotions that occur automatically as reactions to outside events as a result of past associations

B. Memory of skills or behaviors that can be retrieved without conscious awareness

C. Knowledge of the specific events or episodes in your own life history

D. General knowledge about the world that isn't identified with a particular event in your life

E. Memory of facts and events that can be consciously retrieved

F. Memory of highly practiced skills

Memory and the Brain
- Which two areas of the brain are believed to be most involved in long-term memory?

    1.

    2.

Damage to the Cerebellum and Implicit Memory
- If a person has damage to the cerebellum, but no damage to the hippocampus, what would you predict about their memory loss?

PsychSim 5: TRUSTING YOUR MEMORY

Name: _____   **Section:** _____

Date: _____

In this activity you'll be able to test the reliability of your memory, and then learn what researchers have discovered about the way that memories are stored and modified by new information.

Measuring Memory
- According to researchers, what are the three memory processes?

    1.

    2.

    3.

- How do recall tasks differ from recognition tasks?

A Look at Your Performance
- What was your score on the Recall Test? _____
- What was your score on the Recognition Test? _____

Examining Your Performance: Serial Position Effect
- What was your pattern of performance across the 15 words? Did your performance show a serial position effect?

Examining Your Performance: Recall Versus Recognition
- Did your performance show an advantage for recognition over recall?

Examining Your Performance: False Memory

- What is a "false memory?"

- Did you show false recall or false recognition for "sleep"? If so, why do you think this happened? If not, why do you think your performance was different from the Roediger & McDermott study?

Other Ways We Create False Memories

- List and briefly explain the two "sins of forgetting" especially relevant to the topic of false memories:

    1.

    2.

Application: Eyewitness Testimony

- How might memory distortions affect eyewitness testimony?

PsychSim 5: MY HEAD IS SPINNING

Name: _____   **Section:** _____

Date: _____

This activity provides some background information about thinking with verbal concepts versus thinking with mental images.

Conceptual Thinking
- What was your train of thought as you navigated the picture of the candle?

Cooper & Shepard's Results
- In the Cooper & Shepard experiment (1973), participants were asked to decide whether a stimulus (a letter) was normal (simply rotated in the picture plane) or backwards (flipped to its mirror image before the rotation). Reaction times were graphed and increased as the letters were rotated away from 0 degrees. Interestingly, reaction time decreased after 180 degrees. Can you explain why this might occur?

Mental Rotation Experiment
- After completing the Mental Rotation experiment and viewing your data, how would you describe the pattern of your results? Do you think that your results fit the pattern of results from the Shepard experiments?

- After comparing the graphs of your results and the results of the Cooper & Shepard (1973) study, how similar are the two graphs? Did your results show a clear increase in reaction time as the orientation moved away from the vertical? Did your results show a decrease in reaction time as the orientation moved from 180 degrees back to the vertical?

PsychSim 5: DUELING BRAINS

Name: _____   **Section:** _____

Date: _____

This activity examines the research on brain hemispheric specialization and word recognition.

Demonstrating Language Specialization

- What do you think will happen when the computer flashes a word to your left visual field (LVF)? What do you think will happen when the computer flashes a word to your right visual field (RVF)?

   Do you think that one of your hemispheres will be better at reading words? If so, which one?

Word Recognition Task: Your Results

- What were your results? LVF _____   RVF _____

- How would you interpret these results? Did they match your prediction? Did you discover that you "aren't in your right brain when you read?"

Understanding the Right Visual Field Advantage

- Briefly explain why most people show a right visual field advantage on this task.

PsychSim 5: GET SMART

Name: _____   Section: _____

Date: _____

This activity will explore the concept of intelligence and some of the methods of measuring intelligence.

Intelligence and Adaptability
- What does it mean to say that intelligence is a social construct?

- What do two children from dramatically different cultures (a boy working on an arrow and a girl working on a computer) have in common?

Verbal Versus Nonverbal Abilities
- Describe one verbal and one performance subtest of the Wechsler Adult Intelligence Scale (WAIS).

Multiple Intelligences
- Name and describe four of Gardner's eight "intelligences."

Match Sternberg's three "intelligences" with their descriptors:

- o _____ Analytic   A. Problem-solving in everyday tasks

- o _____ Practical   B. Problem-solving in novel tasks

- o _____ Creative   C. Problem-solving in structured, well-defined tasks

Emotional Intelligence
- Define "emotional intelligence."

PsychSim 5: HUNGER AND THE FAT RAT

Name: _____   Section: _____

Date: _____

This activity provides a simulated experiment on weight regulation in rats.

The Hypothalamus
- What are the two techniques used to study hypothalamic dysfunction? How do they differ?

Experimental Simulation
- What conclusions were you able to draw about the effects of the following procedures on the experimental rats:

- Stimulation of the lateral hypothalamus (LH)?

- Destruction of the LH?

- Stimulation of the ventromedial hypothalamus (VMH)?

- Destruction of the VMH?

- What did you learn from this experiment about these two regions of the hypothalamus?

Some Cautions
- What are the two problems with a simple conclusion to this research question?

PsychSim 5: EXPRESSING EMOTION

Name: _____   **Section:** _____

Date: _____

In this activity you will learn about the role of facial expressions in the nonverbal communication of emotion.

Primary Affects

- What emotions are generally considered primary affects? How do they relate to facial expressions?

The Facial Code

- Using the table below, describe the characteristic positions of the eyebrows, eyes, and mouth for each of the six primary affects.

	Eyebrows	Eyes	Mouth
1.			
2.			
3.			
4.			
5.			
6.			

- How does the expression of disgust differ from the other primary affects?

Emotional Blends

- What are emotional blends? How do people generally express them?

Masking Emotion

- How are people able to mask emotions?

PsychSim 5: CATCHING LIARS

Name: _____   **Section:** _____

Date: _____

In this activity you will explore some of the methods used to detect deception.

Nonverbal Cues
- After watching the two video clips, which version do you think is true?

    ____ The first version (born in New York) is true.

    ____ The second version (born in England) is true.

Detecting Emotion from Facial Expression
- After examining the photos, which do you think show a genuinely happy person?

    ____ The left photo shows a genuine smile.

    ____ The right photo shows a genuine smile.

Using a Polygraph to Detect Deception
- Briefly explain how a polygraph is used to detect lies.

Results From the Simulated Polygraph Session
- After you have reviewed the pattern of physiological activity, indicate your best judgment about the truthfulness of the suspect.

    ____ This person is telling the truth. He didn't take the camera.

    ____ This person is lying. He probably took the camera, or knows where it is.

    ____ It's impossible to tell whether this person is lying.

Differences Among the Physiological Measurements

- Why is respiration rate a less reliable indication of nervousness than perspiration or heart rate?

Concerns About the Use of Polygraphs

- Of those listed, which type of error could not be tolerated by the justice system?

PsychSim 5: ALL STRESSED OUT

Name: _____   **Section:** _____

Date: _____

This activity examines the way that psychologists conceptualize stress, emphasizing that stress is a bio-psycho-social process. You will explore the sources of stress in your own life, review your body's response to stress, and then learn how cognitive appraisal dramatically affects how much stress you actually experience.

Checking the Level of Stress in Your Life
- What was your "Stress Test" score? _____

- Do you think that such a test accurately captures your experience? What other stressors should be included?

Stress, Stressors, and Coping
- Psychologists differentiate stressors, strain, and stress. What does each of these terms mean?

The General Adaptation Syndrome
- Describe Selye's general adaptation syndrome.

The Biology of Stress
- Although both men and women experience the fight-or-flight syndrome, some scientists argue that women also can experience stress differently (tend-and-befriend). Briefly explain this hypothesis.

- Can you think of why this alleged gender difference in fight-or-flight and tend-and-befriend may "make sense" from an evolutionary perspective?

- Outline the body's two-part endocrine response to stress.

Stress Harms Your Body's Organ Systems
- List the effects of stress on:

    o   the heart

    o   the digestive tract

    o   the brain

Cognitive Appraisal – The Filter Through Which Stressors Are Processed
- According to the transactional model, what triggers the process of stress?

PsychSim 5: HELPLESSLY HOPING

Name: _____   **Section:** _____

Date: _____

In this activity you will explore the importance of a sense of personal control over the events in your life.

Learned Helplessness
- Briefly describe the animal experiments that lead Seligman to the theory of learned helplessness.

Learned Helplessness and Depression
- What is seen as the conceptual link between learned helplessness in dogs and depression in humans?

Gender and Depression
- Researchers have found that, compared with men, women are twice as likely to develop serious depression. Does the concept of learned helplessness/hopelessness help you understand the gender difference in depression rates?

Personal Control in Everyday Life
- Briefly explain the findings on the importance of personal control in everyday life.

PsychSim 5: MYSTERY CLIENT

Name: _____   **Section:** _____

Date: _____

In this activity you'll take the role of a consultant called in to provide a second opinion on several clients with disorders, based only on the information contained in the clients' files.

This activity will be most useful to you after you have read the text material on psychological disorders.

Psychiatric Diagnosis

- As seen in these five cases, some of the information in a client's files is more useful and relevant than other types of information. Which categories of information did you find most helpful in making your diagnoses?

- Which categories of information did you find least helpful in making your diagnoses?

PsychSim 5: LOSING TOUCH WITH REALITY

Name: _____   Section: _____

Date: _____

This activity explores schizophrenia, one of the most severe and bizarre psychological disorders.

Schizophrenia: A Serious Psychological Disorder
- What are the four behavioral criteria necessary for a person to be classified as having a psychological disorder?

       1.   3.

       2.   4.

Delusions
- What are delusions?

Hallucinations
- What are hallucinations?

Negative Symptoms
- What are negative symptoms of schizophrenia?

Types of Schizophrenia
- Name and briefly describe the three main types of schizophrenia.

       1.

       2.

       3.

Case 1: Identify the Symptom
- Which symptom did she display?

Case 2: Identify the Type of Hallucination

- Can you identify the type of hallucination?

Case 3: Identify the Symptom

- Which symptom did she display?

Case 4-a: Identify the Symptom

- Which symptom did he display?

Case 5: Delusions of Grandeur

- Delusions of persecution or grandeur tend to occur most often in one of the three main types of schizophrenia. Which type is most closely associated with the symptom of delusions?

Case 4-b: Identify Another Symptom

- Which of the five major symptoms of schizophrenia did the young man display in this video segment?

Case 6: Disorganized Speech With Loose Associations

- Loose associations can occur in any type of schizophrenia, but they tend to occur most often in one of the three main types. Which type is most closely associated with the symptom of loose associations?

Case 4-c: Disorganized Speech With Inappropriate Affect

- In your own words, try to describe the symptoms this man is exhibiting in this conversation.

Case 7: Identify the Symptom

- Can you identify which symptom this psychiatric patient displays?

PsychSim 5: COMPUTER THERAPIST

Name: _____   **Section:** _____

Date: _____

In this activity you will engage in a conversation with a "computer therapist," to simulate some principles of active listening from Carl Roger's client-centered therapy.

Computer Therapy

- Think about your "therapy session" with the computer. What limitations did you notice?

- Can you think of any value that a person could obtain from a "therapy session" like this one? Is it possible that a "computer therapist" might offer some benefits that a person may not get from a session with a human therapist?

PsychSim 5: MYSTERY THERAPIST

Name: _____   **Section:** _____

Date: _____

This activity will test your knowledge of the various types of psychotherapy.

The Specific Types of Therapies

- Complete the table below by filling in one main point about each of the eight types of therapy and listing the case number and name of the client receiving that type of treatment.

Type of Therapy	Brief Description	Case Number and Client
Psychoanalysis		
Client-centered therapy		
Systematic desensitization		
Aversive conditioning		
Cognitive therapy for depression		
Family therapy		
Drug therapy		
Electroconvulsive therapy		

Commonalities of Effective Therapies

- As you tried to identify the various types of therapies represented in this activity, did you notice any common themes that ran through all of the therapies?

PsychSim 5: SOCIAL DECISION-MAKING

Name: _____   **Section:** _____

Date: _____

This activity contains a simulation of two classic "social trap" games used in research on competition and cooperation.

Social Decision Making

- As you look back over the past several days, can you think of a decision you made that affected the lives of other people, either in a small way or an important way? Describe it briefly.

Decision Environments

- What is the difference between zero-sum and non-zero-sum environments? Give an example of each.

Zero-Sum Environments

- Explain minimax strategy. In a zero-sum game as demonstrated, a minimax strategy would lead O (the other player) toward which choice? Explain your answer.

- What is a saddle point?

Non-Zero-Sum Environments

- How does trust influence the outcome in a non-zero-sum environment?

- Have you learned anything about your own decision strategies by playing the two trucking games? Explain.

PsychSim 5: NOT MY TYPE

Name: _____   **Section:** _____

Date: _____

This activity explores the process of forming attitudes about other people.

Attribution

- What is the process of attribution?

- What is the fundamental attribution error?

Results of the Rating Exercise

- Do your results show that you formed equivalent attitudes toward the two groups? Or do your results show a systematic bias against one of the groups? If you did show a bias against one group, how would you explain it?

Stereotyping in Everyday Life

- What are stereotypes?

- How are illusory correlations related to stereotyping?

PsychSim 5: EVERYBODY'S DOING IT!

Name: _____   **Section:** _____

Date: _____

This activity explores the issue of social influence—how the behavior of other people affects your behavior.

Social Influence
- What is conformity?

Explaining Sherif's Results
- Why did Sherif's participants change their estimates when they had to call out their answers in the presence of other people?

Explaining Asch's Results
- Why did Asch's real participants deny the evidence of their eyes and report the obviously incorrect answer chosen by the other group members?

Motives for Conformity
- Explain the difference between the two main motives for conformity: informational social influence and normative social influence.

Group Size and Conformity
- What do you think happened in the "Gawker's" study? Can you predict the results?

Resisting Social Influence
- What is reactance?

NOTES

NOTES

NOTES

NOTES

NOTES

NOTES

NOTES

NOTES

NOTES

NOTES

NOTES

NOTES

NOTES

NOTES